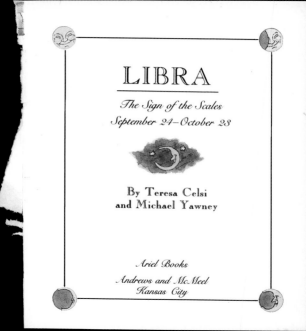

LIBRA

The Sign of the Scales
September 24–October 23

By Teresa Celsi
and Michael Yawney

Ariel Books

Andrews and McMeel
Kansas City

LIBRA

ISBN: 0–8362–3075–2
Library of Congress Catalog Card Number: 93–73369

Contents

Astrology

An Introduction

Early in our history, as human-kind changed from hunter-gatherers to farmers, they left the forests and moved to the plains, where they could raise plants and live-stock. While they guarded their animals at night, the herders gazed up at the sky. They watched the stars circle Earth, counted the days between moons, and perceived an order in the universe.

Astrology was born as a way of finding a meaningful relationship between the movements of the heavens and the events on Earth. Astrologers believe that the celestial dance of planets affects our personalities and destinies. In order to better understand these forces, an astrologer creates a chart, which is like a snapshot of the heavens at the time of your birth. Each planet—Mercury, Venus, Mars, Jupiter, Saturn, Uranus, Neptune, and Pluto—has influence on you. So does the place of your birth.

The most important element in a chart is your sun sign, commonly known as your astrological sign. There are twelve signs of the zodiac, a belt of sky encircling Earth that is divided into twelve zones. Whichever zone the sun was in at your time of birth determines your sun sign. Your sun sign influences conscious behavior. Your moon sign influences unconscious behavior. (This book deals only with Sun signs. To find your moon sign, you must look in a reference book or consult an astrologer.)

Each sign is categorized under one of the four elements: *fire*, *earth*, *air*, or *water*. Fire signs (Aries, Leo, and Sagittarius) are creative and somewhat self-centered. Earth signs (Taurus, Virgo, and Capricorn) are steady and desire material things. Air signs (Gemini, Libra, and

Aquarius) are clever and intellectual. Water signs (Cancer, Scorpio, and Pisces) are emotional and empathetic.

Each sign has one of three qualities—*cardinal*, *fixed*, or *mutable*—which shows how it operates. Cardinal signs (Aries, Cancer, Libra, and Capricorn) use their energy to lead in a direct, forceful way. Fixed signs (Taurus, Leo, Scorpio, and Aquarius) harness energy and use it to organize and consolidate. Mutable signs (Gemini, Virgo, Sagittarius, and Pisces) use energy to transform and change.

Every sign has a different combination of an element and a quality. When the positions of all the twelve planets are added to a chart, you can begin to appreciate the complexity of each individual. Astrology does not simplify people by shoving them into twelve personality boxes; rather, the details of your chart will be amazingly complex, inspiring the same awe those early herders must have felt while gazing up into the mystery of the heavens.

The Sign of the Scales

Libra, the seventh sign of the zodiac, represents relationships. This sign constantly evaluates how everything and everyone connects, compares, and contrasts with other things and people.

Libra's ruling planet is Venus. In mythology, Venus, the Roman goddess of love and beauty, could bring harmony to warring factions and order out of chaos.

Character and Personality

Those born under the sign of the scales always try to balance their seemingly contradictory traits. At times they're lazy, at other times, hard-working. Sometimes they're cool and uninvolved, sometimes they're right in the thick of things. No one trait is allowed to dominate because it would upset this sign's careful balance.

Libras are born diplomats, able to view both sides of a controversy objectively and then negotiate a fair compromise. More importantly, they can find the common ground between opposing sides. With their natural sense of harmony, they bring beauty and order into their environment, which is reflected in their fashion sense and in the artistic way they decorate their homes.

Libra's symbol is the scales, which show its talent for relationships and passion for justice. This sign wants to hear others' points of view and stays neutral in an argument. Libra tries to embody the principles of fairness and balance in its daily life.

When making a decision, Libras weigh every possible course of action and its consequences. This internal debate often causes them to appear indecisive. But the final decision is sure to be the fairest possible.

The Scales are the sign of partnership. Libras don't like to do things alone. To avoid loneliness, they often jump into youthful marriages.

They also tend to follow society's dictates so they won't alienate anyone, fearing they will end up friendless. The exception to this occurs when Libra is upholding a cause it believes is right; then this sign fights courageously, like former British Prime Minister Margaret

Thatcher, nicknamed "The Iron Lady." But most often, the Scales' iron fist wears a velvet glove of charm and wit.

A very social sign, Libra needs to be with others. Since the Scales see people and things in the context of how they relate to one another, Libra's friends and lovers are very important because they give this sign its sense of identity. The Scales will go to any lengths to see that these relationships remain amiable and intact.

For the sake of harmony, this sign usually looks for the best in others. Libra can find something good to say even about the nastiest people. This behavior may seem insincere, but Libra is no flatterer. The Scales just tell the tiny part of truth that is most important to it.

In their quest for a harmonious life, Libras sometimes bottle up negative feelings or conceal their dislike for others. However, the Scales' internal balancing act ensures that repressed feelings will come out in some way—even perhaps in physical illness or unconscious actions.

When Libra understands the value of negative *and* positive feelings in a balanced life and learns how to express them, it is better able to use its natural gifts to bring peace and harmony to others.

Signs and Symbols

Each sign in the zodiac is ruled by a different planet. Libra's planet is Venus, named after the Roman goddess of love and beauty. This sign is symbolized by the scales, which represents balance and harmony.

Libra combines the element of air (intellect) with the cardinal quality of directed energy. Known for its social poise and grace, Libra is a good partner, diplomatic, fair, charming, and sometimes aggressive.

The seventh sign of the zodiac, Libra rules the kidneys, adrenal glands, and lumbar spine. Shades of pink are its colors, opal is its gemstone, and copper is its metal. Libra is associated with Friday and with doves and dolphins. Its lucky number is three.

Trees linked with Libra include the ash and poplar. It rules flowers in general, especially roses, lilies, pansies, and vines. Apples, pears, strawberries, and grapes, as well as wine and sweet desserts, are its foods.

Health and Fitness

ith its natural instinct for balance, Libra understands the need to keep its body healthy. Partner-oriented Libra is inclined to exercise with a friend, preferring to go to the gym with someone rather than work out alone. And social sports involving a small group, like tennis, are preferable to team sports like volleyball.

Sometimes Libras choose food based

When your pattern meets another person's, the two of you might clash or harmonize.

Why this mysterious connection occurs can be explored only by completing charts for both individuals. But even if the chemistry is there, will it be a happy relationship? Will it last? No one can tell for certain.

Every relationship requires give-and-take, and an awareness of the sun sign relationships can help with this process. The sun sign influences conscious behavior. Does your lover catalog the items in the medicine cabinet? Chances are you have a Virgo on your hands. Do you like to spend your weekends running while your lover wants to play Scrabble? This could be an Aries-Gemini combination.

To discover more about your relationship, find out your lover's sun sign and look under the appropriate combination. You may learn things you had never even suspected.

on how it looks rather than on its nutritional value. They also need to curb a sweet tooth. However, no one can balance a diet like the Scales. Those born under this sign instinctively know what to eat to get the right mix of nutrients and vitamins.

Though this sign generally maintains good health, it can be vulnerable in the kidney and bladder areas, as well as the lower back. If Libra represses negative feelings, this could show up in a buildup of toxic wastes. Fortunately, most Libras can tell when their bodies are out of balance and can get help in time.

Home and Family

ecause it seeks beauty in all things, Libra wants to create a peaceful, congenial environment. Its home will be tastefully furnished and arranged.

Just as it arranges furniture, Libra also arranges its family members in the most harmonious combination possible. Family arguments rarely get out of control with the Scales negotiating solutions to problems.

When Libra falls in love, it usually becomes engrossed in its partner. Though family members remain important, Libra's mate is given top priority.

This sign revels in romantic gestures. Libra's ideal mate should celebrate Valentine's Day, birthdays, the first day they met, and any other special occasion with flowers, gifts, candlelight dinners, and festivities on the town.

As a parent, Libra tends to be indulgent. However, its children are expected to say thank you, to play fair, and to be considerate of others.

Careers and Goals

Libras are peacemakers, attracted to any job that allows them to mediate or negotiate, whether it be as a judge, marriage counselor, lawyer, diplomat, psychologist, or referee.

In any profession, Libras work to create harmony and respect for other points of view. And their social sensitivity is especially useful when bringing together people of different customs and cultures.

Ironically, many military leaders, such as Dwight Eisenhower and Alexander the Great, were born under this peace-loving sign. Since Libras see how all things relate to one another, they possess the analytical skills that military leaders need to coordinate supplies, organize troop movements, and understand the enemy.

These tactical skills, combined with Libra's administrative ability, which can cross-reference vast amounts of complex information, should serve the Scales well in most fields.

Pastimes and Play

Taking part in stimulating conversation is Libra's favorite pastime. In fact, the Scales probably have higher phone bills than any other sign.

Games that rely on decision-making ability appeal to Libra, even though this sign may take considerable time to make up its mind when its turn comes around. Partner games also delight the Scales.

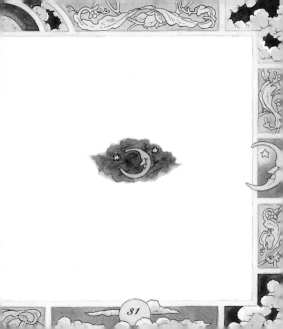

Libra with Aries
(March 21–April 20)

L ibra and Aries represent two opposing approaches to life. Like
other fire signs, Aries is a dar-
ing, vigorous person who is somewhat
selfish. Libra, an air sign, is a contempla-
tive, cautious thinker who always considers the needs and interests of other
people.

Directly opposite each other in the
zodiac, each sign embodies what the

other lacks. Libra and Aries are naturally attracted to each other. Aries' assertive drive is irresistible to the more passive Libra, while the poise and tactfulness of the Scales entice the hotheaded, straightforward Ram. There's a powerful chemistry between these two.

Because of their differences, Libra and Aries have much to learn from each other. From the more diplomatic Libra, Aries can learn to look beyond the purely personal and to be more considerate of others. In turn, Libra can learn much about the value of direct, simple action from the Ram.

Initially, Libra can be swept off its feet by the intense Ram, who knows what it wants and wants it now. But to keep the Scales interested after the first rush of attraction, Aries must learn to slow down, enjoy a candlelight dinner, and take a stroll in the moonlight. Sexually, the Ram takes the spontaneous approach and heads straight for the bedroom. But to Libra, romance is just as important as fiery passion.

Aries always wants top billing, and Libra will put the relationship before anything else, which is good enough for the Ram. When Libra does things to make Aries' life more pleasant, the Ram will accept it all as the treatment it deserves. The self-centered Ram is not accustomed to showing appreciation,

differ in their basic approach to life, they have much to learn from each other.

Emotional Cancer is impressed at how easily the Scales can calm a raging torrent of feeling with just a few diplomatic words. From Libra, Cancer might learn that by distancing itself from feelings, it can make fairer, more impartial judgments. In turn, Cancer could help detached Libra learn to respect emotional truths as well as logical ones.

Sexually, Libra might be amazed at Cancer's intense emotional reactions and tender lovemaking. And Libra's more remote and cool sexuality will fascinate Cancer.

Home and family get top billing with

bra, who finds them too irrational. If this couple can get past their misgivings, they might find enough common ground on which to build a long-lasting relationship.

For instance, both signs fulfill themselves by reaching out to and helping others. They are nurturing, though in different ways. Libra wants everyone to be treated fairly, while Cancer wants everyone to be well fed and happy.

As a water sign, Cancer is sensitive to emotions and hidden motives—so much so that the Crab often feels responsible for the happiness or distress of others. Libra, an air sign, understands the sphere of the intellect better. Because these two

though it should learn how to say thank you and a few other expressions of gratitude to keep Libra happy and to maintain harmony.

If these two get locked into the negative qualities of their signs, Aries can become a bully and Libra can become codependent. But when the relationship works, Aries teaches Libra to become more assertive, especially when voicing its needs, and the Scales instruct the Ram in diplomacy and appreciation of the finer things in life.

Each balances the excesses of the other. As long as they respect and accommodate those differences, this couple could have a lifetime of love.

Libra with Taurus

(April 21–May 21)

Both Libra and Taurus are slow to commit to a relationship: Libra has to weigh every aspect of the decision, and Taurus doesn't like to change. But both have similar goals in life and a strong desire for harmony. For Libra, harmony is achieved with beauty and order; for Taurus, a sensual earth sign, harmony comes from experiencing the physical world to the fullest—in other words, feeling good.

For example, Libra selects a sofa for the living room based on its color and style; the Scales want the couch to work with the size and the colors of the room. Taurus will simply sit on the couch to see how comfortable it is.

Libra may mistake Taurus's deliberateness for laziness. Taurus may think Libra is too picky. But since neither sign likes to argue, they'll make every effort to smooth over conflicts.

Sometimes, however, the way these two deal with disagreement can be frustrating. Libra loves a stimulating debate, which helps it find a middle ground. Not

Taurus. The Bull cares more about dinner than debating and will give in easily. This tendency to concede the point can be frustrating to Libra who likes resolution.

When the Bull *does* argue, its opinions and arguments can be too dogmatic and heated for the detached examination of the Scales. Libra often evades this kind of argument, leaving Taurus as frustrated as Libra.

Another difficult area is old versus new. Taurus craves the old and familiar: friends, clothes, food, restaurants. Libra loves new challenges and change and may get fed up with stodgy Taurus.

This potential conflict can be an advantage if the Scales broaden Taurus's world and the Bull provides a stable nest where Libra can entertain new friends. And, if Taurus doesn't care for the social whirl Libra so enjoys and would rather stay home and watch a video, Libra must remember it's okay to leave your partner at home sometimes.

Both signs prefer slow, romantic lovemaking. Taurus's sensual, calm nature reassures Libra when life goes too fast. The Bull appreciates the refinement of Libra's romantic ways.

Realistic Taurus offers idealistic Libra tenderness, security, and sensuality. This could be the perfect balance for the Scales.

Libra with Gemini

(May 22–June 21)

Loaded with charm, style, and good looks, this popular and entertaining couple seems made for each other. Though Libra and Gemini rarely have a grand passion, they share enough affection and understanding to keep the party going for a lifetime.

In Gemini, Libra discovers a quicker, more energetic version of itself, and

balance. Libra's constant need to feel secure as a couple might cause it to become clinging. Possessiveness is unnerving to Gemini, who needs personal space within a relationship.

Communication is one of this couple's strongest assets. As long as they can discuss their needs for security and independence, they should be able to resolve problems. And if they can achieve a balance between togetherness and freedom, they can have the best of both worlds: companionship of a true soul mate and the mental freedom of an undemanding relationship.

Libra with Cancer
(June 22–July 23)

hen two warm, sentimental signs meet, falling in love should be easy. But when Libra and Cancer get together, mistrust might keep them apart.

Libra's smooth charm puts the self-protective Crab on guard—it suspects an ulterior motive. Cancer's strong emotional reactions scare off the logical Li-

Gemini finds someone more socially graceful. Since both play by their wit and charm and quickly size up each other's game, they will feel freer and more open as a team.

Love for these two air signs is more in the mind than the heart. Libra loves being in love with love but resents heavy emotional demands, so the Scales are thrilled to meet someone who is equally affectionate yet shares its distaste for complicated emotions.

In this cerebral relationship ideas take center stage. These two discuss and debate everything with endless fascination. Even in the bedroom, they express love verbally as well as physically. For them, sex is a delightful pastime rather than an expression of ardent passion.

If these signs live together, their home will be a convivial place, full of guests and drop-in visitors. Both need an active social life, though Gemini may prefer larger gatherings than Libra. However, compromise comes easily to those born under the sign of the Twins, so this minor difference rarely grows into a major disagreement.

Harmonious as it is, this relationship has some conflicts. Both of these signs like the newest in fashion, ideas, and gossip. But Gemini's restless, exhausting search for stimuli—especially for other people—can throw the Scales off

This sign spends a lot of energy making its world more beautiful. Libra enjoys the arts, especially concerts and films that can be shared with others. Shopping is also an artistic outlet: clothes, antiques, whatever—Libra will spend hours evaluating the attractiveness and value of every object it sees.

Literary Libras love fine writing. Detective stories and courtroom dramas, in which the villain is caught or sentenced at the end, satisfy their desire for justice. Of course, romances of all kinds, with plenty of stylish details, are particular favorites.

Love Among the Signs

What is attraction? What is love? Throughout the centuries, science has tried and failed to come up with a satisfying explanation for the mysterious connection between two people.

For the astrologer, the answer is clear. The position of the planets at the time of your birth creates a pattern that influences you throughout your lifetime.

Libra with Pisces

(February 20–March 20)

ithout some outside force to bring them together, Libra and Pisces might pass by each other, like ships in the night. They often meet on a blind date or at the office, because neither sign would initiate a relationship on its own.

Once these two do meet, they'll realize they behave in similar ways, even if they have different motivations. For

of communication. Neither is interested in sex merely for its physical pleasures. Whatever problems they may have in other areas of their relationship, everything goes smoothly for them in the bedroom. Libra brings out the hidden romantic side of Aquarius, and the adventuresome Water Bearer has some delightful surprises for Libra.

Understanding and love come easily to these two. If they can deal with their differences in the daily business of life, such as paying bills, shopping for food, and cleaning house, they may have found a good combination of friend and lover.

derlying stresses in their relationship. At first, this couple usually has a strong mutual admiration. Libra is attracted to Capricorn's decisiveness and ambition, while the Scales' charm and conversational skills dazzle the more reserved Goat. They share a strong interest in culture and are likely to enjoy exploring museums or going to concerts together.

But the Capricorn reserve is tough for even the most probing Scales to crack. The Goat hides its feelings and resists any attempt from Libra to charm or seduce. Capricorn gives nothing away, unless it's sure it will get something back—and that includes emotions —while Libra happily spends its emotional energy to create a harmonious atmosphere.

This couple's fondness for tradition should bring them together. Both love an old-fashioned sentimental courtship that allows plenty of time to get to know each other and develop trust. In time, as trust develops, a deeper communication may result.

One main area of tension is that both Libra and Capricorn want to be the boss. As cardinal signs, each feels he or she is the rightful leader. And they're correct—both are natural leaders and poor followers. To keep from clashing, each should take charge of a different area of the partnership.

Sexually, these signs will blossom in a committed relationship. Though Capricorn is reserved, this earth sign gets more open and adventuresome as time goes on. Libra will be pleasantly surprised as the Goat becomes increasingly expressive of its passion.

If this couple can resolve their emotional and power issues, they'll make an excellent team. Libra will create the beautiful, traditional home of Capricorn's dreams, and the Goat will provide security and direction for the Scales. And the rewards awaiting the couple that pulls through difficult challenges will greatly enrich both their lives.

Libra with Aqu

(January 21–Febru

U npredictable,
ius could th
permanentl
that might be just w

Both love the s
Aquarius likes to ble
while Libra prefers
tact. They're likely
the office, where th
the social games

keep their options open to other people,
which gets in the way of commitment.
Lifestyle differences present other
challenges. For example, erratic Aquarius will sleep fourteen hours one night
and two the next and eat at a different
time and place each day. The Scale
should forget about countering the
ter Bearer's unpredictability.

Another problem for this c
getting projects off the groun
discuss where and how to d
maybe even draw up pla
it's time to take actio
back. Outside help
these two to reali
For this pa

Libra with Capricorn
(December 22–January 20)

oth Libra and Capricorn are traditionalists who thrive on courtship rituals. Whether they are kissing on the doorstep, meeting the future in-laws, or taking vows in a church, these two will imitate the roles of lovers they've seen in the movies or read about in books.

The perfection with which they play their parts, however, could hide the un-

tarius's restlessness, the Archer might feel smothered and flee.

This couple is sure to share a love life that varies from playful to passionate to tender. Their ever-changing moods reflect the ever-changing emotions that pass between them.

A cool air sign, Libra is encouraged by Sagittarius's fiery enthusiasm to take risks and have a more stimulating lifestyle. And the logical, charming Scales could be the perfect bull's-eye for the restless Archer.

than fight back, but it might swim off if it gets too many orders.

No matter who's boss, neither of these two is good at making decisions. Libra has to debate all sides of any issue, even if it is ordering dinner, and Pisces, who would rather not make any decision, will be satisfied with whatever dish Libra orders.

Sexually, these two click since both love romance. Libra wants flowers and candlelight dinners, and Pisces never forgets a birthday or Valentine's Day.

But even if these two fall deeply in love, there will be problems. Pisces needs emotional involvement with a variety of people and seeks out new experi-

example, Libra is kind to others because it wants to be liked or wants to do the right thing. Pisces is kind because it naturally empathizes with others.

Unfortunately, air sign Libra and water sign Pisces may never really understand what makes the other tick. Mystical Pisces acts on intuition and deep, subtle feelings that cannot be expressed. Libra acts after logically weighing all the pros and cons, then spells everything out in plain language.

If they do get together, these signs must decide who is going to take the helm. The sign of the Scales prefers to steer the relationship with tact and diplomacy. Pisces is more likely to give in

Libra with Leo
(July 24–August 23)

L eo wants to be the center of the universe—and Libra is the sign most likely to put the Lion there. For all Leo's vanity and self-centeredness, this sign could be one of the best partners Libra could find.

The attraction is simple: Each partner provides just what the other needs and desires. Leo likes to be the focus of attention and admiration. That suits Libra

these two signs. If they decide to marry, they will probably agree on a traditional wedding and seek their families' approval. Cancer is more concerned with financial security than Libra and might manage the couple's financial and business affairs.

Libra's plans and dreams will infuse optimism into Cancer's outlook, while the Crab's willingness to face harsh truths can give Libra the reality check this sign needs. A fair exchange!

Libra's analytical skill is added to Leo's confident selling power.

As a fixed sign, Leo doesn't care for change, which, over time, could make lovemaking seem routine to Libra. However, Libra's ardent response to the Lion's fiery passion could encourage them into varying their pleasures.

Libra tempers the self-centered and aggressive aspects of Leo, while the Lion's stability steadies the vacillating Scales. In Libra's endless quest for balance, Leo is one of the best possible partners.

Libra with Virgo

(August 24–September 23)

Virgo, like the famous Virgo Greta Garbo, often wants "to be left alone." Thus it might seem an unlikely match for Libra, who idealizes partnership. But these signs have much in common and often admire one another's differences.

In the beginning, Libra could easily write off Virgo as dull. Outwardly, Virgo seems like one of the least roman-

charm, and style could round out serious-minded Scorpio.

To stay together, however, both signs must understand their basic differences. Libra is open and sociable; Scorpio is mysterious and private. Libra is optimistic; Scorpio is suspicious and slow to trust others. When wronged, Libra seeks justice—Scorpio seeks revenge.

Libra may be astonished at the intensity of Scorpio's opinions and desires. The Scorpion is extremely decisive, sure of what it likes and what it wants. Scorpio may see Libra's constant deliberation as a sign of weakness, while Libra may consider Scorpio's harsh judgments unfair.

Scorpio's emotions run deep; yet because it does not indulge in flowers, compliments, or sweet talk, Libra could wrongly conclude that the Scorpion does not care. To please romantic Libra, Scorpio should try to be more demonstrative. And Libra should try to understand the unconventional ways that Scorpio expresses its emotions.

Sexually, Libra's cool elegance and Scorpio's intense passion will be a good mix, at first. Later, Scorpio may find the Scales' cerebral approach lacking, while Libra might find the emotional Scorpion too much of a good thing.

Libra will have to tone down flirtations with the opposite sex, however

fine since this sign enjoys applauding others. The magnanimous Leo rewards admirers with undying loyalty, which is just the kind of devotion Libra longs for.

Both Libra and Leo are romantics, in love with love. When the Lion radiates warm affection and dramatically declares its feelings, reserved Libra gives its heart more easily than ever.

However, Leo must receive continual attention, and the Scales will be responsible for providing a steady stream of solicitude to satisfy Leo. Libra must be careful, however, not to deny its own needs or to idealize bold, dashing Leo.

Libra can best hold its own by using

its natural tact and diplomacy to influence the Lion gently and subtly. Proud Leo never minds making changes, as long as it doesn't feel like it is giving in.

These two will probably share an extravagant lifestyle, indulging their tastes for the finer things in life. Libra loves everything beautiful and refined, and Leo loves to go first class all the way. Money arguments will probably be over which luxury to buy rather than over how much to spend.

Though it sounds like these two will be headed for the poorhouse, often the reverse will be true. These signs are able to combine their talents to make money as easily as they spend it, especially when

tic signs of the zodiac. This earth sign is too busy dealing efficiently with the real world to indulge in flattering or flirting, like Libra. Down-to-earth Virgo considers all that Libra hearts-and-flowers business silly and somewhat wasteful.

However, beneath the Virgin's diffident exterior lies a romantic heart that is best won through serious talk. Virgo analyzes everything. This sign knows how each shot contributes to a film's total effect and how each special-interest group affects a political process. The Scales, who naturally examine all sides of any question, will be thrilled by the stimulating debates these signs can have. Rather than having a candlelight dinner,

the ideal evening for this pair might
hashing over current events or analyzin
a new book. This might not fully satisf
Libra's romantic side, but it will work.

These two signs have similar ob-
sessions: Virgo's neatness plays into
Libra's orderliness, and they'll constantly straighten up after each other.
Both have a strong drive to serve their
partner and are eager to please each other
sexually. In fact, the ease with which
these two share a home makes this relationship look easier than it is.

Some predictable differences may
pose problems as the relationship deep-
ens. Virgo is not very social; Libra is
extremely social. Virgo is a specialist,

Libra a generalist. The Virgin, a perfectionist, is compelled to criticize, while the Scales hate any discord. Virgo has a strong independent identity, separate from its partner; Libra's identity centers on a partner.

To avoid mutual resentment, these two intelligent signs must find a way to be true to themselves while pleasing each other. If they are willing to compromise, this could lead to a dynamic and satisfying relationship between equals.

foreign policy to the best way to fix a sink. However, these two debaters may never actually decide on anything. With other signs, Libra is pressed for some kind of action—not so with another Libra. They can spend hours deciding where to eat dinner or what film to see, and still never get to the restaurant or the movie theater.

These lovers' sexual styles blend perfectly. Both are selfless and attentive. As satisfying as sex may be, it is not central to Libra's happiness. More important are affectionate rituals, like a peck on the cheek before leaving for work, a birthday card, unexpected flowers—these are vital to the Scales.

Libras are so giving that this relationship may lack the spark and challenge of romance with one of the more self-motivated signs. However, the emotional fulfillment and easy companionship that two Libras offer each other can make it well worthwhile. And with their social skills, this couple can attract plenty of friends to provide the variety their relationship may lack. Interesting projects and shared goals can give this pair a sense of direction and broaden their horizons—together.

Libra with Scorpio

(October 24–November 22)

T hough they seem to live in two different worlds, the fascination that Libra, a logical air sign, and Scorpio, a deeply emotional water sign, have for each other is strong.

Libra longs for a forceful love, one that can provide a clear sense of direction. Proud, passionate Scorpio could fill the bill. In turn, Libra's positive attitude,

frivolous they may be, to avoid Scorpio's jealousy. Loyalty is of utmost importance to Scorpio, who is always on guard against any sign of betrayal.

Tension can occur because Scorpio tends to insist that Libra pour all its emotional energy into the relationship, even though Libra enjoys the fun and stimulation of a wide circle of friends. However, both signs value a committed relationship. If Scorpio can control its possessiveness and allow Libra some breathing room, and if Libra can be more emotionally demonstrative to Scorpio, this couple might have a long-running romance.

Libra with Sagittarius

(November 23–December 21)

L ibra's heart will proclaim that Sagittarius is the one worth waiting for, even if the freedom-loving Archer keeps the Scales waiting a long time.

This is a terrific combination. Open communication is the big plus in this relationship. Sagittarius is able to elicit from Libra substantial discussions rather than charming chatter. Too often, Libra tells its partner what he or she wants to hear. But because the Archer values honesty, it is easy for Libra to respond openly and directly.

Libra is delighted that the Archer always has some stimulating new idea to debate. And Sagittarius, a natural philosopher whose ideas are constantly evolving, will benefit from Libra's analytical mind.

Libra's fairness and Sagittarius's generosity blend well. Together, they radiate warmth and interest in others, helping them move easily through their wide-ranging social world. While Sagittarius inspires respect and affection, it lacks Libra's tact. The Scales find the Archer's frequent social blunders mortifying. Usually, however, Libra's diplomatic skills can smooth things over.

Tensions might develop if Sagittarius's need for freedom conflicts with Libra's need to be part of a couple. Even though neither will be threatened by the other's flirting or the reappearance of an ex-lover, Libra may worry that Sagittarius will run off in search of adventure. But the Archer won't necessarily rove or be gone long if it does. And if Libra's charming companionship is not suffocating, the Archer will miss the Scales and be back all the quicker. On the other hand, if Libra is not sensitive to Sagit-

Libra with Aquarius

(January 21–February 19)

Unpredictable, exciting Aquarius could throw Libra's scales permanently off balance—and that might be just what Libra needs.

Both love the social scene, though Aquarius likes to blend with large groups, while Libra prefers more individual contact. They're likely to meet at a party or the office, where they'll both be observing the social games and the players.

Sexually, these signs will blossom in a committed relationship. Though Capricorn is reserved, this earth sign gets more open and adventuresome as time goes on. Libra will be pleasantly surprised as the Goat becomes increasingly expressive of its passion.

If this couple can resolve their emotional and power issues, they'll make an excellent team. Libra will create the beautiful, traditional home of Capricorn's dreams, and the Goat will provide security and direction for the Scales. And the rewards awaiting the couple that pulls through difficult challenges will greatly enrich both their lives.

Since both are intellectual air signs, Libra will immediately relate to Aquarius's detachment, which can make the Water Bearer seem cold to most people. When they interact, both signs, though courteous, may seem uninvolved with each other. Disagreements will be discussed rationally, but on those rare occasions when they fight, they'll throw reason out the window and give in to blind fury.

It is a common pattern for Libra and Aquarius to break up, then make up. As air signs they understand each other, but Libra wants a relationship that's like a peaceful breeze while Aquarius likes to churn up a storm. And they both like to keep their options open to other people, which gets in the way of commitment.

Lifestyle differences present other challenges. For example, erratic Aquarius will sleep fourteen hours one night and two the next and eat at a different time and place each day. The Scales should forget about countering the Water Bearer's unpredictability.

Another problem for this couple is getting projects off the ground. They'll discuss where and how to do something, maybe even draw up plans. Then, when it's time to take action, both will pull back. Outside help will be necessary for these two to realize their dreams.

For this pair, lovemaking is a form

LIBRA

This Book Belongs To

_____